ABUNDANT TRUTH INTERNATIONAL MINISTRIES

Abundant Truth International's Inspirational Series

OUT OF THE PIT INTO PURPOSE

Discovering Hope and Freedom in the Christian Journey

Roderick Levi Evans

Out of the Pit into Purpose
Discovering Hope and Freedom in the Christian Journey

All Rights Reserved © 2011 by Roderick L. Evans

No part of this book may be reproduced or transmitted in any form or by any means, graphic, electronic, or mechanical, including photocopying, recording, taping, or by any information storage or retrieval system, without the permission in writing from the publisher.

Front & Back Cover Designs by Abundant Truth Publishing

Abundant Truth Publishing
an imprint of Abundant Truth International Ministries

For information address:
Abundant Truth International
P.O. Box 126
Camden, NC 27921

Unless otherwise indicated all of the scripture quotations are taken from the Authorized King James Version of the Bible. Scripture quotations marked with NIV are taken from the New International Version of the Bible. Scriptures marked with NASV are taken for the New American Standard Version of the Bible.

ISBN 13: 978-1601415417

Printed in the United States of America.

Contents

Introduction

Chapter 1 – Why Me? The Self-Defeating Question   1

Problems of Life   3
Patience of Job   4

Chapter 2 – The Art of Endurance in the Christian Life   9

Endurance brings Stability   12
Endurance Guards and Revives   13
Endurance Guarantees Success   14
Endurance is a Prerequisite   16

Contents (cont.)

Chapter 3 – Whose Report will You Believe? 19

Ask 24
Expectation 25
Glory 26

Chapter 4 – Overcoming Frustrations in the Christian Life 31

The Truth of God 35
The Plan of God 36
The Peace God 37

Chapter 5 – Exposing the Deception Called Doubt 43

Keep a Watchful Eye 45

Contents (cont.)

Keep the Word of Truth   47

Keep an Honest Heart   49

Chapter 6 – Seal the Record   53

The Problem of "Real"   57

Deliverance Declarations   58

Chapter 7 - The Road to Everlasting Life   63

The Ultimate Purpose   65

Four Directional Signs   67

Bibliography   73

Introduction

The Christian life is simple and complex simultaneously. Its simplicity rests upon one truth: Jesus Christ is the Son of God and that faith in Him results in man's salvation. However, to live a fruitful Christian life comes from navigating through the complexities of life. The Abundant Truth Inspirational Series was developed to aid the Christian in handling the difficulties that come with the Christian experience.

In this Publication

In this book, we have compiled select teachings and exhortations to transform the Christian's walk with Christ. Some areas of interest are overcoming and endurance. Also, exhortations in overcoming self-defeating questions. It is our prayer that every Christian will come out of personal pits and achieve 0their God-given purposes.

-Chapter 1-

Why Me?
The Self-Defeating Question

OUT OF THE PIT INTO PURPOSE
Discovering Hope and Freedom in the Christian Journey

Well, here we are again: another day, another problem, another issue confronting me!

Problems of Life

Sometimes, things can go wrong for so long that your outlook on life can become bleak. Many end up asking the timeless, self-defeating question... "Why Me?"

Why died I not from the womb? why did I not give up the ghost when I came out of the belly? Job 3:11 (KJV)

As Job went through his testing... his outlook on life turned from joy into utter despair. It got so bad until he wished he were never born. Though some will not admit it, even Christians who know the Lord experience these types of feelings. Though they might surface, the Christian still has to know that he is not alone and that God will deliver.

Patience of Job

We know from further reading of Job's story that the Lord did deliver him and rescue him from his troubles and pains.

Ye have heard of the patience of Job, and have seen the end of the Lord; that the Lord is very pitiful, and of tender mercy. James 5:11 (KJV)

God showed great compassion to Job because of his sufferings. He will do the same for Christians today. Know that though your tests and trials are numerous and painful that God has not left you and will show you graciousness. Be encouraged knowing that in the end, God will show you peace, favor, and give you rest.

OUT OF THE PIT INTO PURPOSE
Discovering Hope and Freedom in the Christian Journey

OUT OF THE PIT INTO PURPOSE
Discovering Hope and Freedom in the Christian Journey

Notes:

_____

_____

_____

_____

_____

_____

_____

OUT OF THE PIT INTO PURPOSE
Discovering Hope and Freedom in the Christian Journey

_____

_____

_____

_____

_____

_____

_____

_____

_____

-Chapter 2-

The Art of Endurance in the Christian Life

OUT OF THE PIT INTO PURPOSE
Discovering Hope and Freedom in the Christian Journey

In athletics, there are events that measure success by the speed, strength, and ability. However, there are events, which are a matter of endurance, rather than pure skill or ability. In many of the strongman competitions, certain events not only require skill, but endurance.

Not only must the competitor be able to lift or carry the weight, but also they have to do it for a sustained amount of time. Thus, their ability to lift or carry becomes secondary to being able to endure the weight. The same applies to the Christian today.

We learn the scriptures and spiritual truth, but many do not know how to endure hardships and challenges. We gain skill, knowledge, and understanding, but in the time of testing do not last.

Endurance brings Stability

Every Christian has to learn The Art of Endurance as they grow in God's grace and knowledge. Without endurance, the Christian can possess spiritual insight and knowledge, but cannot last long enough to see the fruits of it flourish in life.

There are defining aspects to the Art of Endurance. The Christian, who understands these, will be successful in their walk with Christ.

Endurance brings stability during uncertain times. Endurance helps one to maintain their pursuits in this life in the midst of adversities. Endurance helps one to see beyond the pain and see the promises of Christ and the hopes and dreams of tomorrow.

Endurance Guards and Revives

Endurance guards against the desire to quit. Endurance has the motto that "Quitting is not an Option," which stifles the desire to give up and quit.

Endurance helps to revive faith. Endurance gives the user a since of faith. Endurance causes an individual to remember the Word of God and His personal promises.

Endurance brings the believer closer to perfection in Christ. Endurance causes an individual to look past hurts, disappointments, and ungodly desires. Thus, bring a greater level of purity, morality, and holiness in Christian living.

Endurance Guarantees Success

Endurance is a guarantee of success in spiritual warfare. Endurance causes believers to outlast every attack of the enemy. One of his tactics is to cause believers to let down their guards and allow him to dominate their lives. But, if the Christian endures, the warfare of the enemy will not accomplish what it is sent to do.

Yes. Life does bring problems, both great and small. Sometimes, hardships and trials can last for years and it seems as if there will be no end. However, remember the Art of Endurance. It will be worth it in the end. Remember, our walk with Christ has promise in this life and in the life that is to come.

Endurance is a Prerequisite

Endurance is a prerequisite to eternal salvation. Jesus stated that the one, who endures to the end, shall be saved. He did not say the one who did more or knew more. Thus, one major aspect of endurance is that it guarantees entrance into eternal life.

OUT OF THE PIT INTO PURPOSE
Discovering Hope and Freedom in the Christian Journey

Notes:

OUT OF THE PIT INTO PURPOSE
Discovering Hope and Freedom in the Christian Journey

_____

_____

_____

_____

_____

_____

_____

_____

_____

-Chapter 3-

Whose Report will You Believe?

Understanding the Power of Faith in God

OUT OF THE PIT INTO PURPOSE
Discovering Hope and Freedom in the Christian Journey

To believe or not to believe is the question at hand. Foundational to the Christian life is the ability to have faith; that is, believe. Without a belief in the work of God through Jesus Christ, one cannot enter into salvation.

Moreover, the obtained salvation cannot be maintained without an ever-growing faith, hope, and belief in God. Our belief in God has to go beyond a general belief in His existence. It has to expand to a solid belief in His power and ability to move on the behalf of man.

And straightway the father of the child

cried out, and said with tears, Lord, I believe; help thou mine unbelief. Mark 9:24 (KJV)

Why is it hard at times to maintain an unwavering faith God? Even after He has done so many things apparently, it can still be difficult to trust Him. Many believe and do not believe, simultaneously. They know that God answers prayer and can do all things, but the breakdown is that they do not believe that God will do it for THEM.

Many Christians do not struggle with believing in God's existence or His ability to act. However, they do not trust or believe that God will act on their behalf. Many are crippled by this type of erroneous thinking. Causes for this thinking vary from individual to individual. Some do not believe because they do not think they deserve anything from God.

Others feel that they have done so much wrong that God could not possibly hear their requests. And yet, others feel that if they are not in a position of authority in the Church (pastor or a leader of some kind) that they are not on God's radar. All of these thoughts are inconsistent with sound Christian thought and practice.

Here are 3 reasons why a Christian should not lose their belief in God's power to act on their behalf. Consider these the next time you feel as if your prayers may not be answered.

Ask

He told us to ask. Jesus encouraged His disciples in the parable of the woman and the unjust judge to pray. He said that we are to always pray and not faint.

The parable He used demonstrated that even though we may have to pray about a situation more than once, it does not mean we will not get our request. We should come to Him in prayer, again, because He said so. He gives an open invitation. Why not receive it?

Expectation

He told us to ask in expectation. Unless something is just outside of His will, we can expect to receive what we ask for.

He said that everyone that asks, receives. Jesus said that if our earthly fathers knew how to give good things, how much more our heavenly Father. If you are brave enough to ask, He is big enough to perform it.

Glory

He told us to ask so God would receive glory. Jesus told the disciples that anything that they asked for in His name, He would do it that the Father may receive glory. When we ask and God does it, we give Him glory and tell others of His good works towards us. God receives no glory in unanswered prayers. Trust that He will do it for you.

The next time you approach God in prayer. Do not doubt His willingness to hear you. If it is not in His will, He has a way of revealing that even to you. Aside from that, come to Him in faith, expecting to receive. Remember, He offers forgiveness in prayer, healing in prayer, and answers so that one can stand in Him. To believe or not to believe it is up to you.

Notes:

_____

_____

_____

_____

_____

_____

_____

_____

OUT OF THE PIT INTO PURPOSE
Discovering Hope and Freedom in the Christian Journey

_____

_____

_____

_____

_____

_____

_____

_____

_____

-Chapter 4-

Overcoming Frustrations in the Christian Life

In military action, they have covert operations. These are military campaigns, which are done undercover to surprise and subdue the adversary. In Christianity, there is a covert operation in place by the adversary; that is, frustration. Frustration is an inevitable part of life; even the Christian life.

Frustration surfaces because life does not stop. Even those that have faith in God can sometimes sink into this pit of discouragement, depression, and despair. The words of David become the hallmark of existence,

My God, my God, why hast thou forsaken me? Why art thou so far from helping me, and from the words of my roaring? Psalms 22:1 (KJV)

Have you ever wondered: Why does God allow us to suffer? Why does He seem so uninterested at times to our supplications and prayers? It feels as if He does not care about what we are going through.

We know from David's words and the words of Christ on the cross that it happens in the life of those who possess faith in God.

We may not always understand why or receive an answer from Him about why we have to go through so many bad things. Yet, we must maintain our faith, hope, and trust in Him. To master frustration, we want to leave three points of consideration. If you remember these, you will do well.

The Truth of God

First, God is not a liar. Though it may seem as if God has forsaken you and left you alone, He gave a promise saying that He will never leave you, nor forsake you. Even when it seems like He is not there, He is. His presence is the only reason you have not quit or had a breakdown. He is there.

The Plan of God

Second, God has a plan and purpose in all things. It does seem insensitive when someone says to us that God has a plan when we are experiencing devastating situations: such as death, sickness, loss of job, and other life changing events.

It seems this way because we forget that ultimately, God's plan revolves around the souls of men and their salvation rather than a person's personal comfort.

We may not always agree, but God is love and wants what is best for us. Either negative circumstances can draw us closer to Him or we can allow them to push us away from Him. In addition, God's plan may be that others see your faith in the midst of your trials and troubles, which brings glory to Him.

The Peace God

Third, God gives peace. Jesus promised His disciples peace. He told them that they would have problems, but His peace and joy would be with them. Some Christians do not recall this. God gives peace and joy because we will experience hardships and difficulties.

The problem is that we focus on God changing the situation, rather than on the fact that He can give peace, joy, grace, and strength while we go through it. The peace of God is available, but we have to ask for it, receive it, and walk in it.

Though frustration surfaces, it does not have to master us. We can trust His love; knowing He will do justly in our lives. Continue to believe, hope, and trust knowing that frustration does not have to be your lot. You can foil your frustrations before they dominate you.

OUT OF THE PIT INTO PURPOSE
Discovering Hope and Freedom in the Christian Journey

Notes:

OUT OF THE PIT INTO PURPOSE
Discovering Hope and Freedom in the Christian Journey

_____

_____

_____

_____

_____

_____

_____

_____

_____

-Chapter 5-

Exposing the Deception Called Doubt

OUT OF THE PIT INTO PURPOSE
Discovering Hope and Freedom in the Christian Journey

When we consider the word, "deception," oftentimes false doctrines and cult leaders enter into the mind. As Christians, we are taught to be on guard against deception.

Keep a Watchful Eye

Thus, we have watchful eyes as it pertains to biblical teachings and self-proclaimed ministers and miracle workers. However, there is a type of deception that many Christians are submitting to consistently; that is, the deception of doubt. It is one of the main reasons why we doubt the promises of God.

If you ask your average Christian, they will tell you that they are not deceived. This assertion is based solely upon their belief system and possibly their denominational affiliation. Yet, when a Christian fails to believe God and what He has said in His word, they are deceived. The devil is the father of lies. Nothing that he says in rooted in truth. Even when he uses the truth, it is twisted that the plan of God will be thwarted.

He used the scriptures during Christ's temptation in the wilderness to get Christ to operate in a manner not purposed by

God. The enemy uses the same tactics today. He will bring scriptures to mind to make us doubt God and what He will do for us.

Keep the Word of Truth

God is truth. Even Jesus declared that He was the way, the truth, and the light. In God, there is no variableness or shadow of turning; that is, He does not change. He remains consistent to who He is.

This means that we should be able to trust in Him and His plan for our lives. In addition, we should be ale to trust His love, care, and concern for us. Even in the direst situations, we can declare God's faithfulness and His ability to deliver us.

Consider this: if God is unchanging and He has given us promises and He cannot lie; not to believe Him is a consequence of deception. The deception of doubt causes you to mistrust the One who is truth.

When you feel that you cannot trust God and wait upon Him, you are deceived because He said that we could count on Him. He stated, "I will never leave you, nor forsake you." God is not faithful because we are always faithful, but He is faithful because He cannot deny Himself.

Keep an Honest Heart

Are you operating in deception today? Are the situations in your life that you are unsure of what the Lord will do? Do you feel that God has forsaken you? Do you feel that God can no longer use you because of failures? Do you think God will be there for others and not for you? If your answer to any of these is "Yes," then you are deceived. However, there is hope.

Confess to God that you have had a difficult time believing, and ask for strength and grace to overcome the deception of doubt. Finally, move in faith, knowing that He will be with you, even until the end of the world. In Christ, the promises of God are "yes" and "amen."

Notes:

_____

_____

_____

_____

_____

_____

_____

_____

OUT OF THE PIT INTO PURPOSE
Discovering Hope and Freedom in the Christian Journey

-Chapter 6-

Seal the Record

OUT OF THE PIT INTO PURPOSE
Discovering Hope and Freedom in the Christian Journey

The foundation of any established organization is good bookkeeping. And, a sign of good bookkeeping is confidentiality. In the government, when certain events took place, though they maintain internal records, they sealed them from view in external records. These files are not open to the general public or general inspection.

In essence, what they are saying is that the events that took place are between them and the involved party. The question maybe asked, "What does this have to do with our overcoming fears?"

And he closed the book, and he gave

it again to the minister, and sat down. And the eyes of all them that were in the synagogue were fastened on him. Luke 4:20 (KJV)

The answer is simple: There are many people in the Body of Christ who need to seal the book on past sins and failures; and in some cases, on present struggles and weaknesses.

Some people are fearful of repercussions of their pasts and keep reliving it over and over again. It comes up in the form of "would have, could have, and should have."

The Problem of "Real"

Yet, there is another group who feel that in order to be "REAL" they need to expose past indiscretions and present struggles. However, wisdom is needed in this regard because two negative outcomes may manifest:

1. Exposing present weaknesses invites unnecessary temptations and trials. Some people have opened up to individuals for help and were taken advantage of, or they were ridiculed and belittled.

2. Some people use exposing present weaknesses as an invitation to sin. Be

careful of people who tell you they can trust you with their innermost details. Sometimes they are sharing with you to give you a personal invitation into ungodliness. You need to tell them to "Seal the Record."

Deliverance Declarations

The reason we can seal the record is because of what Jesus did when He entered the synagogue and read from Isaiah. He opens the book and reads a fivefold description of the deliverance He offers.

1. Preach to the Poor – Those who feel the least in this world can be made rich through the knowledge of Him.

2. Heal the Brokenhearted – Those who have been emotionally scarred, bruised, and hurt can be liberated.

3. Preach deliverance to the Captives – Those who are captive to lifestyles, mind-sets, and even people can be freed through Him.

4. Recovery of sight – Those who have been blinded by sin and the devil can gain spiritual sight and insight so that they can understand who they are in Him.

5. Set at liberty the bruised – Those who are trodden down and wearied by life

and suffering from all matter of afflictions can be set free through Him.

After Jesus' reading, the text tells us that He closed the book. By interpretation, it reveals that His work of total deliverance is complete if we receive it. Jesus already closed the book.

Do not stay in jail when the door has been opened. Again, Seal the Record on things of the past, present struggles, and future worries because faithful is He that is called you and He will also do it.

OUT OF THE PIT INTO PURPOSE
Discovering Hope and Freedom in the Christian Journey

Notes:

OUT OF THE PIT INTO PURPOSE
Discovering Hope and Freedom in the Christian Journey

_____

_____

_____

_____

_____

_____

_____

_____

_____

-Chapter 7-

The Road to Everlasting Life

(The Ultimate Purpose)

OUT OF THE PIT INTO PURPOSE
Discovering Hope and Freedom in the Christian Journey

Everyone is on a road to an eternal destination. In life, different roads can be taken on a journey to reach a particular destination.

The Ultimate Purpose

Though we can compare our walk with Christ as a journey, there is only one way to reach our destination of heaven. You cannot enter into the kingdom of God any which way you choose. Remember, it is the ultimate purpose of your Christian journey.

Enter ye in at the strait gate: for wide is the gate, and broad is the way, that leadeth to destruction, and many there be which go in thereat. Matt 7:13 (KJV)

Some promote the ideology that you do not need to go to church; that is, fellowship with other Christians or even receive Christ to enter into heaven.

But, as Christians, we must stand on the truth that reception of Christ, fellowship with other Christians, and striving to live a life pleasing to Him is a perquisite for entrance into heaven.

With the advent of personal GPS devices, people no longer have to depend on standard maps to reach their destinations. Now, they can pick and choose the route that they would like to take, rather than standard routes. This is fine for personal travel. However, this phenomenon has taken on spiritual implications.

Four Directional Signs

In the Church, individuals are now using "spiritual" GPS systems to determine how they will live for Christ and enter into heaven. They forsake the road map of Christ and those things that are written. Many times, the "GPS" used is based upon feelings and intellectual reasoning which is causing many to deviate from the path set before men by Christ's example and exhortations of scripture.

The scriptures verify that life is a journey. Here are 4 signs (among many) that we must pay attention to as we are on the Christian journey.

1. Stop – Certain activities are inconsistent with the Christian life. To live in sin is not an option. We can stop (overcome) sin while we live in this life.

2. Detour – Sometimes, we must learn to do things differently. Detours come up

to show us that a path that was once acceptable is no longer accessible.

3. Yield – This sign prepares you to slow down. As Christians, we have to slow down and yield to direction and inspiration of the Spirit.

4. Road Work Up Ahead – We have to be prepared for God's pruning and maturing process in our lives. As Christian, we must know that spiritual road work is up ahead as we live for Him.

We must be committed to a successful journey. Remember to pay attention to the spiritual road signs. In doing so, you will have success as a Christian in this life and with joy, you will enter into the life that is to come.

Notes:

OUT OF THE PIT INTO PURPOSE
Discovering Hope and Freedom in the Christian Journey

_____

_____

_____

_____

_____

_____

_____

_____

_____

Bibliography

Lockman Foundation. *Comparative Study Bible.* Zondervan Publishing House. Grand Rapids, MI, c1984

The Bible Library. *The Bible Library CD Rom Disc.* Ellis Enterprises Incorporated, (c) 1988 – 2000. 4205 McAuley Blvd., Suite 385, Oklahoma City, OK 73120. All Rights Reserved.

Merriam-Webster Online Dictionary. Copyright © 2005 by Merriam-

Webster, Incorporated. All rights reserved.

Notes:

OUT OF THE PIT INTO PURPOSE
Discovering Hope and Freedom in the Christian Journey

www.ingramcontent.com/pod-product-compliance
Lightning Source LLC
Chambersburg PA
CBHW050343010526
44119CB00049B/676